Gabriele Koch

# Gabriele Koch

© 1995 and 2002 Marston House.
Introduction Sir David Attenborough

**Marston House**

First edition published 1995, second edition 2002

Published by Marston House,
Marston Magna, Yeovil BA22 8DH, UK
**in association with Alpha House Gallery
Sherborne, Dorset**

ISBN 1899296-16-6

Illustration on p. 2: Height 40 cm, 1999
Right: height 78 cm, 1997

Typeset by Remous Ltd
Printed in China by Regent Publishing Services

# **Introduction** by Sir David Attenborough

Elemental. The dictionary says that means 'of or pertaining to the four elements'. And what are they? According to classical philosophy – earth, water, air and fire. Gabriele Koch's lovely pots speak of all four of those elements as vividly as any I know.

Like all pots, being of clay, they are of the earth. They have the contours produced by water when it smooths a boulder in the bed of a stream; or by sand-blasting winds that over thousands of years chamfer the cliffs of a desert. Fire? No pots show more clearly than hers the caress of the kiln and the lick of flame and smoke.

Why should elemental qualities in pots bring such profound pleasure? Some might suggest that such a response is merely the sentimental reaction of urban aesthetes who have been cut off from the realities of the natural world. I have proof that it is not so. Only the other day, I was admiring another pot with qualities remarkably similar to those that come from Gabriele's hands. It had that same in-turned lip, that same swelling contour – half-egg, half belly – and smoky clouds swirling over its surface. But it also carried a clear indication that the potter who made it took pleasure in its shape and texture for he – or more probably she – had enhanced both with five incised rings around its mouth. And she had done so, somewhere on the plains around the Mississippi, a thousand years ago.

Another dictionary provides another definition of that word – elemental. 'Motivated by and symbolic of powerful natural forces or passions,' it says. Gabriele Koch's pots are indeed elemental. In every sense.

# Einleitung von Sir David Attenborough

Elementar – „Teil der vier Elemente oder diesen zugehörig", sagt das Wörterbuch. Und welche sind diese vier Elemente? Nach dem Verständnis der klassischen Philosophie – Erde, Wasser, Luft und Feuer. Gabriele Kochs wunderbare Gefäße sprechen von jedem dieser vier Elemente so lebendig wie nichts sonst, das ich kenne.

Wie alle Gefäße aus Ton, gehören sie der Erde an. Sie haben Konturen, die das Wasser schafft, wenn es im Flussbett einen Stein glatt schleift, Formen, wie sie die sandhaltigen Winde in Jahrtausenden aus dem Felsgestein der Wüste herausschälen. Feuer? Keine Gefäße verraten deutlicher als ihre die Liebkosung des Brennens, das Lecken von Flammen und Rauch.

Warum verschaffen uns diese elementaren Qualitäten, wenn wir sie in Gefäßen vorfinden, eine so tiefe Befriedigung? Manche sehen in solchem Genuss nur eine sentimentale Reaktion urbaner Ästheten, die sich von der Wirklichkeit der Natur abgeschnitten fühlen. Ich habe den Beweis, dass dem nicht so ist. Vor kurzem habe ich ein anderes Gefäß bewundert, das in seinen Eigenschaften auf bemerkenswerte Weise denen ähnelte, die von Gabrieles Hand stammen. Es besaß denselben einwärts gebogenen Rand, dieselbe typisch gewölbte Silhouette – halb Ei, halb Bauch – und Schattierungen, die wie Rauchwolken über seine Oberfläche wirbelten. Doch es ließ auch deutlich erkennen, dass der Töpfer, der es schuf, Gefallen gefunden hatte an seiner Form und Oberfläche, denn er – oder höchstwahrscheinlich sie – hatte beides mit fünf um die Öffnung eingravierten Ringen verziert. Und sie hatte diese Arbeit vor rund tausend Jahren irgendwo in den Flussebenen des Mississippi ausgeführt.

Ein anderes Wörterbuch liefert uns eine weitere Definition des Wortes „elementar": „bestimmt von und symbolisch für mächtige Naturkräfte oder Leidenschaften", heißt es. Gabriele Kochs Gefäße sind in der Tat elementar. In jeder Hinsicht.

# Gabriele Koch

*An appreciation by Tony Birks*

In her mother's house in Germany there is a pot by Gabriele Koch, a brown vessel which would be at home alongside a collection of African or Pre-Columbian art. It has an affinity with anonymous utilitarian tribal pottery, burnished with use. This was an early work, c. 1982, by this remarkable contemporary artist. It embodies the spirit of hand-building, the source of Gabriele's first inspiration. Like the very earliest potters, she used, and still uses, the coiling technique, which requires no equipment at all, just the skill of hand and eye. It is a primitive technique, but it is not self-limiting. In regard to form and scale, it is a much more flexible and amenable technique than working on the wheel. It allows the artist great freedom, and the opportunity to build pots of prodigious size.

Gabriele Koch chose this basic technique, and her own way of developing it, but the work that has flowed from her hands over the last twenty years has moved away from the ethnic pots of her early exhibitions. She first gained her reputation with organic forms - enclosed shapes, tight and luscious as apples, but not *like* fruit or vegetables because of her precise control of the radial symmetry. Making a truly symmetrical pot by coiling is very difficult, and needs an immense amount of practice and a sculptor's eye. Gabriele employs both, and the test of this symmetry is to set one of her large vessels spinning on its tiny base like a stately

Diam. 32 cm
1982

Jupiter or Saturn, without the hint of a wobble.

In the last few years the focus of her work has turned towards more sharp-edged forms, with complex curving planes. Perhaps this may be to do with her interest in architecture, which dates from her childhood in Germany. Her enlightened parents would take her on trips to see modern buildings like the Ronchamp chapel, where sculptural form is expressed architecturally. In later years she came to love the sculptural aspect of the built environment in peasant villages in Spain, and to appreciate mud-brick built settlements in Africa, Latin America and India. Here new houses are built room by room according to need, and functional aesthetics without all the impedimenta of European architectural tradition produce pure form which this potter took to her heart.

She also responds to the inventive iconoclasm of modern architects such as Daniel Liebekind and Frank Gehry, whose Vitra Design Museum building is near to the South German town of Lörrach where Gabriele was born.

She left Germany for England in 1973, and her pottery training in this country began in the next year. It was a good time to come. The influential Goldsmiths' College where she later studied was in full flow, and several talented potters were emerging in an atmosphere where discipline rubbed shoulders with freedom of expression. Gabriele's first one-man show was in London in 1984 and by the year 2002 she had held twenty-nine solo exhibitions in this country and abroad, and her reputation extends beyond Europe. Her work is in over twenty public collections, including the Victoria and Albert Museum and the Sainsbury Centre for Visual Arts, and is increasingly valued.

Because of the labour-intensive nature of her technique, she can only produce a limited number of pots per year. The studio where she works without assistants will normally contain five or six pots at various stages, and it is here that the form and the surface texture is controlled and completed. The method Gabriele uses she describes herself in the following pages. The final patterned surface, with what appears to be several layers of luminous colour is not made in the studio. It is the outcome of a slow second firing in sawdust, in which oxygen starvation and the mixture of different types of timber dust both play a part.

The sawdust firing is very low-tech, but is carefully organised, and there are inherent dangers to the fabric of the pot through steep temperature gradients. With her long experience and not a little experimentation Gabriele now has few failures in the sawdust kiln.

Cloud formations growing up through air currents provide a thrill for the eye. So do the patterns created on Gabriele's pots, deftly guided through a temperamental and sometimes fickle fire. Because of the process, no one pot can ever be the same as another in pattern or in colour.

So much for the surface: finally the form. A pot is a membrane between an inside space and an enclosing space. Gabriele's work can be seen in terms of the tension between the two, and in some more recent forms she has been emphasizing the relationship between the inner and outer spaces either with small orifices, slits and cuts, thus revealing the substance of the pot, and leading the eye inside, or by creating double-skinned forms where the void between inner and outer surface tests her skills both aesthetically and technically.

In this she is sharing an agenda with certain modern sculptors, notably Rachel Whiteread and Anish Kapoor, and it is not a surprise that she also admires the work of Richard Serra and Eduardo Chillida. And there is a sculptor's response to the work of Gabriele Koch: one of her early collectors is Sir Anthony Caro.

Height 23 cm
2001

# Gabriele Koch

*Eine Betrachtung von Tony Birks*

In Gabriele Kochs Elternhaus in Deutschland steht einer ihrer Töpfe, ein braunes Gefäß, das in einer Sammlung Afrikanischer oder Vorkolumbianischer Kunst zu Hause sein könnte. Es ist der anonymen Gebrauchstöpferei von Stammesgesellschaften verwandt, durch Handhabung glatt poliert. Das war eine frühe Arbeit, etwa um 1982, dieser bemerkenswerten zeitgenössischen Künstlerin. Es verkörpert die Seele handgeformter Gefäße, von denen Gabriele ihre erste Anregung schöpfte. Wie die Töpfer der Frühzeit baute sie damals wie heute noch ihre Gefäße mit Tonwülsten auf, was keinerlei Werkzeug erfordert außer der Geschicklichkeit von Hand und Auge. Es ist eine primitive Technik, die den Künstler jedoch nicht eingrenzt. Mit Hinsicht auf Form und Größe ist sie viel anpassungsfähiger und besser zu kontrollieren als die Arbeit an der Töpferscheibe. Sie erlaubt dem Künstler große Freiheit und ermöglicht ihm, Gefäße von erstaunlichem Umfang zu bauen.

Gabriele Koch hat diese ursprüngliche und einfache Technik gewählt und auf ihre eigene Art und Weise entwickelt, aber die Arbeit, die in den letzten zwanzig Jahren unter ihren Händen entstand, hat sich von den ethnischen Töpfen der ersten Ausstellungen entfernt. Sie hat sich zuerst einen Namen mit organischen Formen gemacht – eingeschlossene Volumen, straff und üppig wie Äpfel, aber nicht Obst oder Gemüse gleichend auf Grund ihrer präzisen Kontrolle der Radialsymmetrie. Es ist sehr schwer, ein wirklich symmetrisches Gefäß von Hand aufzubauen und es bedarf einer ungeheuren Menge Erfahrung und des Auges eines Bildhauers. Gabriele verfügt über beides, und diese Symmetrie lässt sich dadurch testen, dass man eines ihrer großen Gefäße auf seiner winzigen Standfläche rotieren lässt, wie einen prächtigen Jupiter oder Saturn, ohne dass es auch nur im Geringsten schwankt.

In den letzten Jahren hat sich ihre Arbeit neuen Formen mit schärferen Kanten und kompliziert gewölbten Flächen zugewandt. Möglicherweise ist das auf ihr Interesse an Architektur zurückzuführen, das sie schon in ihrer Kindheit in Deutschland entwickelt hat. Ihre aufgeschlossenen Eltern haben oft Ausflüge gemacht, um ihr moderne Gebäude wie die Kirche von Ronchamp zu zeigen, wo skulpturelle Form architektonisch ausgedrückt ist. Später begeisterte sie sich für das skulpturelle Erscheinungsbild der Bauweise spanischer Dörfer und entwickelte eine starke Bewunderung für Lehmbauten in Afrika, Lateinamerika und Indien. Hier werden Häuser je nach Bedarf Zimmer für Zimmer gebaut, und ungehindert von der Bürde einer europäischen Architekturgeschichte schafft diese funktionale Ästhetik reine Form, die sich diese Keramikerin zu Herzen genommen hat.

Sie reagiert auch positiv auf die kreative Bilderstürmerei moderner Architekten wie Daniel Liebekind und Frank Gehry, dessen Gebäude des Vitra Design Museums ganz in der Nähe von Gabrieles Geburtsort Lörrach in Süddeutschland steht.

Sie kam 1973 nach England und begann im Jahr darauf ihre Keramikausbildung. Sie hatte einen guten Zeitpunkt gewählt. Das einflussreiche Goldsmiths' College, wo sie säter studierte, erlebte in jener Zeit eine ungewöhnlich kreative Phase, und in der Atmosphäre jener Jahre, in der Disziplin und Freiheit des persönlichen Ausdrucks Hand in Hand gingen, traten mehrere talentierte Keramiker in Erscheinung.

Gabriele hatte ihre erste Einzelausstellung 1984 in London. Bis zum Jahre 2002 hat sie ihre Arbeit in neunundzwanzig Einzelausstellungen in England und im Ausland vorgestellt und sich über Europa hinaus einen Namen gemacht. Ihre Arbeiten sind in über zwanzig öffentlichen Sammlungen vertreten, u.a. dem Victoria und Albert Museum und dem Sainsbury Centre for Visual Arts, und werden von einer wachsenden Zahl von Sammlern geschätzt.

Weil ihre Arbeitsweise sehr zeitaufwendig ist, kann sie nur eine begrenzte Anzahl von Gefäßen pro Jahr anfertigen. In ihrer Werkstatt, wo sie ohne Gehilfen arbeitet, stehen gewöhnlich fünf oder sechs Gefäße in verschiedenen Fertigungsstadien. Hier kontrolliert und perfektioniert sie ihre Form und Oberflächenstruktur. Gabriele beschreibt ihre Arbeitsweise selbst auf den folgenden Seiten. Die endgültige Oberflächenmusterung, die wie mehrere Schichten leuchtender Farbe erscheint, entsteht außerhalb der Werkstatt. Sie ist das Resultat eines langsamen, zweiten Brandes in Sägespäne, wo Sauerstoffmangel und die Mischung verschiedener Sorten von Holzspäne eine Rolle spielen.

Der Rauchbrand ist sehr „low-tech", d.h. technisch primitiv, aber er wird sorgfältig vorbereitet, und wegen der starken Temperaturschwankungen ist die Struktur des Gefäßes unvermeidlichen Gefahren ausgesetzt. Auf Grund ihrer langen Erfahrung und umfangreicher Experimente hat Gabriele nun relativ wenig Verlust beim Rauchbrand.

Wolkenbilder, die durch Luftströmungen entstehen, versetzen den Betrachter in Erregung. Dasselbe passiert bei den Mustern von Gabrieles Gefäßen, die geschickt durch ein launisches und zuweilen unberechenbares Feuer geführt werden. Wegen dieses Brennvorgangs ist jedes Gefäß in Muster und Farbe einzigartig.

Kommen wir zur Form. Ein Gefäß ist die Membran zwischen einem inneren und einem umschließenden Raum. Man kann Gabrieles Werk als Ausdruck der Spannung zwischen beiden sehen, und in einigen ihrer jüngeren Arbeiten hat sie die Beziehung zwischen Innen- und Außenraum entweder durch kleine Öffnungen, Schlitze und Einschnitte betont, wodurch sie die Substanz des Gefäßes enthüllt und das Auge nach innen führt. Oder sie hat doppelwandige Formen geschaffen, wo der Hohlraum zwischen der inneren und äußeren Oberfläche ihre Geschicklichkeit in ästhetischer als auch technischer Hinsicht auf die Probe stellt. In diesem Punkt trifft sie sich mit einigen zeitgenössischen Bildhauern, vor allem mit Rachel Whiteread und Anish Kapoor. Es überrascht daher nicht, dass sie auch das Werk von Richard Serra und Eduardo Chillida bewundert. Tatsächlich liegt auch eine Reaktion aus der Reihe der Bildhauerei auf das Werk von Gabriele Koch vor: Einer ihrer ersten Sammler ist Sir Anthony Caro.

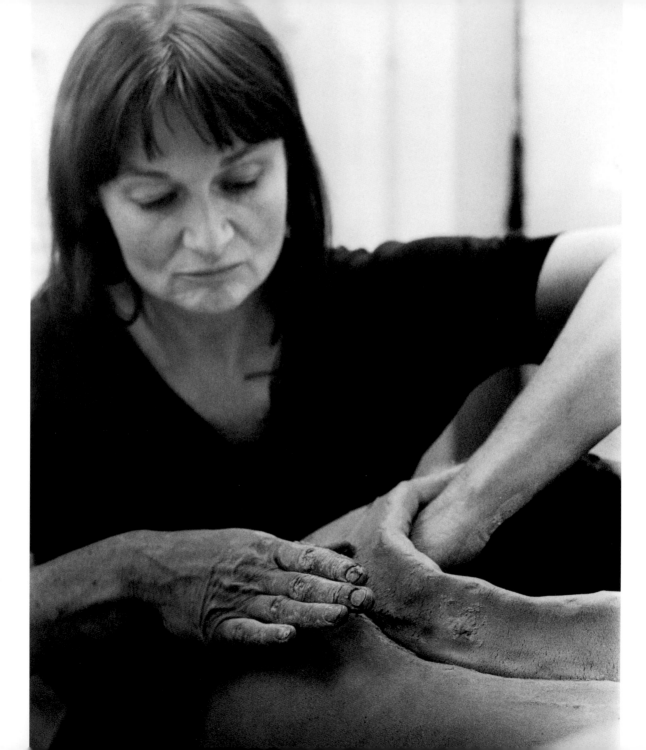

# Ceramic method

*Gabriele Koch describes her technique*

I mainly use one clay. It is the white-firing refractory clay called 'T' Material, popular with hand builders. It contains grains of molochite grog of regular size. I buy it ready prepared, but wedge it thoroughly before starting to build. Sometimes I mix with other clays.

For most of my work the initial form is a bowl, which I pinch to shape. Sometimes, if I am making a tall form with a flat base, will I cut out a disc for the base from rolled out clay. Pinching a bowl shape gets the form started and establishes, too, the thickness of the pot's walls.

I start the coil by rolling the clay vertically between my hands and then I lay it on the bench, rolling it thinner with my fingers before I flatten it with a series of regular taps using the side of my hand. Thus, for a fairly substantial pot a single coil applied as a ring to my pinched bowl base will give an increase of about 3–4 centimetres in height, while the thickness of the wall is not more than one centimetre. I have to be able to control the form perfectly, and I can only do this if the clay is at exactly the right stage of dampness. I put another coil on top of the previous one, having scratched the top of the lower one with a metal knife, and brushed it with thick 'T' Material slip for adhesion. I complete the join on both sides of the wall with upward and downward pressure of the fingers, and sometimes I will add a very fine coil on the outside where the two main coils meet to ensure that the join is really strong.

I normally leave the pot to dry somewhat after every coil but to preserve a damp surface where the next coil is to be added I place a damp strip of cotton cloth around the perimeter. If the pot is going to be a swelling bowl form, I would rest the base on a bowl deeper than the shape of my base – a cereal bowl or something like that, lined with cloth. This allows me to manipulate the pot on a banding wheel easily while giving it some support. I prefer to allow the clay to dry naturally, but it can be speeded up by the careful use of a blow-torch on the softer areas.

Hand building is inevitably a slow process, and those who rush any of the stages generally come to grief. It is for this reason that I have several forms on the go at once – by moving from pot to pot I can keep working without a break – I have to attend to different stages in the various pieces I am working on. To control the form I use a beating tool – usually a wooden spoon – on the outside, with a hand for support on the inside. I use a metal kidney as a scraper when the clay is drier. Closed-in forms – spherical or near spherical shapes – are very strong, but an open form like a shallow bowl tends to be floppy and needs much support. Whatever I am doing, controlling the dryness of the clay is always in my mind, and when the shape itself is finished I will sponge the surface to raise the tooth of the clay before applying my slip.

The slip is prepared from the clay body, sieved to remove the molochite grog, and coloured with oxides and body stains. I am always experimenting with slip coloration in an attempt to produce rich deep colours which are not chalky, and it is not easy, as slips only develop a richness of colour when under a transparent glaze, which of course I do not use. I can only say with confidence that iron oxide is a reliable old friend, but I do use other oxides and a variety of body stains. I am not a chemist, and tend to try out the materials offered by ceramic suppliers, adding to the clay up to about 30% of the dry weight. I paint the slip on to a still-damp pot as a very thin cream, and usually do this in two stages up to twelve hours apart – bottom first, top afterwards. This is because the wet slip so softens the thin-walled form that shapes can become flabby or even sag out of control if the slipping is done as a single operation.

The burnishing process begins when the slip is drying but not bone dry. It has to be damp enough to compact under pressure from my burnishing tool (usually the back of an old teaspoon), but not so damp that it moves about or adheres to the spoon. Burnishing does take a long time, with a regular circular pressing motion to give the surface an even sheen, and

I am told that each potter who uses the burnishing technique will make a distinctive and personal pattern or patina. I usually burnish the surface three times, twice while it is rather damp, and finally as it becomes drier before the biscuit firing.

The biscuit kiln is taken slowly to a maximum of 950°C – above that temperature the shine disappears and thus most of the effort of burnishing would be wasted. When the forms come out of the biscuit kiln they look rather naked to me because I am so used to the effect of a second firing in a sawdust kiln. It really does not matter what kind of kiln is used for the biscuit. I use gas but oil or electric kilns are just as good. It is only necessary to control the temperature rise carefully.

A reliable kiln with an accurate pyrometer nowadays means modern technology; the sawdust kiln I use for the second firing is the opposite. It is a dustbin or an oil drum with sawdust placed below, around, inside and above the pot, and lit from the top. I use a blowtorch to fire up the sawdust because I don't want it to go out. There is nothing magical about the blowtorch or about the speed at which the sawdust burns down around the pot. The tricky bit, which gives the pattern, is the way in which the sawdust is packed against the pot and how the pot itself is arranged. The markings are the result of the darkening of the body clay underneath the slip when the fire draws oxygen from the clay to assist the combustion. Smoke and the patterning of the pot will only happen where the pot is in contact with combustion. There are of course numerous variations in the extent and coverage of smoking according to the angle at which the pot is placed in the sawdust. If the pot is removed before the firing is complete the smoking will be arrested, but such removal has to be done with care, with tongs and refractory gloves. I avoid tongs if possible because they can mark the pot. Rapid cooling is not good, and I prefer to leave the pot in the sawdust for up to 24 hours after the firing is complete. If the pot is taken out from the kiln as it still burns, like a raku pot, it is vital to control the rate of cooling by wrapping it in a thermal blanket covered in tinfoil.

Only when it is quite cool do I wash it in water with a soft cloth or sponge to make it clean and reveal the pattern. It is quite an exciting moment! The final stage is a light coating of wax polish which brings up the sheen of the burnished surface like old leather. My technique is a very slow and laborious process, and it is not recommended for people who are impatient for quick results. But there is a steady rhythm in the work, and it can be both demanding and soothing at the same time.

# Arbeitsweise

*Gabriele Koch beschreibt, wie sie arbeitet*

Ich arbeite hauptsächlich mit T-Material, einer weiß brennenden Tonmasse, die sich für das Aufbauen von Gefäßen besonders gut eignet. T-Material enthält eine feine Molochitkörnung, die dieser Tonmasse ihre Festigkeit verleiht. Ich kaufe den Ton im Fachhandel bereits fertig aufbereitet, knete ihn aber vor Arbeitsbeginn gründlich durch. Manchmal mische ich noch andere Tonsorten bei.

Ich fange die meisten Gefäße mit einer von Hand geformten Schale an. Wenn ich jedoch eine hohe Form mit flachem Boden baue, schneide ich eine runde Platte aus dem flach ausgerollten Ton aus. Wenn ich mit einer von Hand geformten Schale anfange, treffe ich schon weitgehend die Entscheidung über den weiteren Verlauf der Rundung des Gefäßes und den Durchmesser der Gefäßwand.

Bei der Herstellung von Tonwülsten rolle ich den Ton zuerst senkrecht zwischen den Händen und rolle ihn dann weiter auf der Werkbank aus. Zuletzt schlage ich ihn mit der Seite meiner Hand in regelmäßigen Abständen zu einem flachen Band. Dieses Band setze ich als durchgehenden Ring an die ursprüngliche Schale an und erreiche damit für ein ziemlich großes Gefäß einen Zuwachs von etwa 3–4 Zentimetern, während die Gefäßwand höchstens einen Zentimeter dick ist. Ich muß die Form vollkommen unter Kontrolle haben und dazu muß die Feuchtigkeit des Tones genau richtig sein. Ich setze das nächste Band auf das vorhergehende an, nachdem ich die Oberfläche des letzten Bandes mit einem Messer kreuzweise eingeritzt und mit dickem Tonschlicker bestrichen habe, damit die beiden Berührungsflächen gut zusammenhaften. Ich verwische die Ansatzstelle, indem ich den Ton auf beiden Seiten mit dem Daumen nach oben und unten streiche. Manchmal arbeite ich eine sehr feine Tonwulst in die äußere Fuge, um sicherzustellen, dass die beiden Bänder wirklich gut zusammengesetzt sind.

Nach jedem neu angesetzten Band lasse ich das Gefäß etwas antrocknen. Damit der obere Rand, an den das nächste Band angesetzt werden soll, feucht und weich bleibt, lege ich einen feuchten Streifen Stoff darüber. Wenn ich ein Gefäß mit rundem Boden baue, stütze ich den Boden auf dem Rand einer Schale ab, die tiefer ist als die Rundung meines Gefäß-bodens. Damit sich der Rand der Schale nicht zu sehr in den noch etwas weichen Ton eindrückt, lege ich etwas Frottierstoff dazwischen. Das ermöglicht mir auch, das Gefäß auf der Ränderscheibe von allen Seiten zu bearbeiten, da es sich mit dem Stoff leicht auf der Schale verschieben lässt. Es ist besser, wenn man den Ton an der Luft trocknen lässt, aber man kann diesen Vorgang etwas beschleunigen, indem man die weicheren Stellen mit einer Lötlampe vorsichtig etwas anwärmt.

Wenn man von Hand aufbaut, ist das immer ein langsamer Arbeitsprozess. Versucht man, irgendeinen dieser Arbeitsgänge rasch zu erledigen, rächt sich das meistens später.

Deshalb arbeite ich an mehreren Stücken gleichzeitig – indem ich erst an einem und dann am nächsten Gefäß arbeite, vermeide ich Wartepausen und verschaffe mir Abwechslung, da ich auf diese Weise meistens mit mehreren verschiedenen Arbeitsstufen beschäftigt bin. Ich behalte die Form unter Kontrolle, indem ich die Außenseite mit einem Klopfwerkzeug – gewöhnlich einem Holzlöffel – bearbeite, während ich die Innenseite mit der linken Hand abstütze. Wenn der Ton etwas angetrocknet ist, benutze ich eine gerundete Ziehklinge, um die Innenseite sauber zu schaben. Gefäße mit einer kleinen Öffnung haben die endgültige Oberflächenbehandlung nur auf der Außenseite. Eine fast geschlossene Rundform ist ziemlich stabil, aber eine offene Form – wie z.B. eine flache Schale – neigt dazu, zusammenzufallen und muss daher gut abgestützt werden. Woran ich auch arbeite, ich muss immer die Feuchtigkeit des Tones im Auge behalten. Wenn ich die Form eines Stückes fertig gestellt habe, rauhe ich die Oberfläche mit einem feuchten Schwamm etwas auf, bevor ich meine Engobe auftrage.

Die Engobe besteht aus dem Ton, den ich für den Aufbau des Gefäßes benutze. Ich siebe die Molochitkörner aus und mische gegebenenfalls Oxide und Farbkörper bei. Ich experimentiere ständig mit der Einfärbung von Engoben und versuche dabei, tiefe, warme Farben zu bekommen, die nicht kreidig aussehen. Das ist nicht so einfach, denn Engoben entwickeln ihre volle Leuchtkraft erst in Verbindung mit einer transparenten Glasur, die ich aber nicht benutze. Ich weiß mit

Sicherheit, dass ich mit Eisenoxid zuverlässige Resultate erziele, aber ich verwende auch andere Oxide und eine Reihe von kommerziell hergestellten Farbkörpern, die ich auf 100 Gramm Trockengewicht Ton bis zu etwa 30 Prozent beimischen kann. Ich trage die Engobe mit einem Pinsel in dünnflüssiger Form auf das noch feuchte Gefäß auf. Das passiert normalerweise in zwei Arbeitsgängen mit bis zu zwölf Stunden Pause dazwischen – erst der untere Teil, dann der obere Teil. Das ist notwendig, weil die feuchte Engobe die dünnwandige Form so aufweicht, dass straffe Formen ihre Spannkraft verlieren oder ganz in sich zusammensacken können, wenn die ganze Engobe auf einmal aufgetragen wird.

Die Polierarbeit beginnt, wenn die Engobe trocknet, aber bevor sie lederhart ist. Sie muss genug Feuchtigkeit enthalten, um sich unter dem Druck meines Polierwerkzeugs (meistens die Unterseite eines Löffels) zusammenzupressen, darf aber nicht so feucht sein, dass sie schmiert oder am Löffel kleben bleibt. Polieren ist eine zeitraubende Arbeit, bei der ich in regelmäßiger Kreisbewegung der Oberfläche einen gleichmäßigen Glanz verschaffe. Es scheint, dass jeder Töpfer, der diese Poliertechnik anwendet, ein ganz eigentümliches und persönliches Muster oder Oberflächenbild erzeugt. Ich poliere die Oberfläche in der Regel dreimal – zweimal, wenn sie noch relativ feucht ist, und zum Schluss, wenn sie schon weiter getrocknet ist, vor dem Schrühbrand.

Der Schrühbrand wird langsam auf eine Höchsttemperatur von 950°C gebracht –

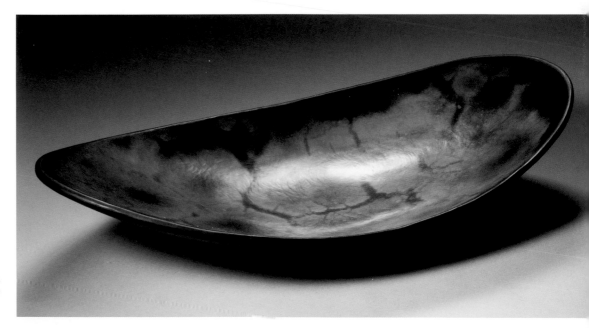

Length 64 cm
2000

brennt man höher, verschwindet der Glanz und damit hätte man die ganze Polierarbeit fast umsonst gemacht. Wenn die Arbeiten aus dem Schrühbrand kommen, erscheinen sie mir fast etwas nackt, weil ich so an die Wirkung des Zweitbrandes in Sägespäne gewöhnt bin. Es macht keinen Unterschied, welche Art von Brennofen für den Schrühbrand benutzt wird. Ich habe einen Gasofen, aber ölbeheitzte Brennöfen oder Elektro-Öfen gehen genau so gut. Es ist nur wichtig, dass der Temperaturanstieg sorgfältig überwacht wird. Ein zuverlässiger Brennofen mit einem genauen Pyrometer bedeutet heutzutage moderne Technologie; der Sägespäneofen, den ich für den Zweitbrand benutze, ist das genaue Gegenteil – ein Mülleimer aus Metall oder eine große Öltrommel. Ich fülle erst den Boden mit Sägespäne und dann den ganzen Bereich um und über dem zu brennenden Gefäß, das selbst auch mit Sägespäne gefüllt ist. Dann zünde ich das Ganze von oben an. Ich benutze ein Lötlampe, um das Feuer gut in Gang zu bringen, denn es darf nicht wieder ausgehen. Die Lötlampe oder das Verbrennen der Sägespäne an sich sind kein Zauberkunststück. Das Geschick, das die Musterung beeinflusst, liegt in der Art und Weise, in der die Sägespäne um das Gefäß gepackt ist und wie das Gefäß selbst platziert wird. Die Markierungen sind das Ergebnis der Dunkelfärbung des Tonkörpers unter der Engobe, wenn das Feuer dem Ton Sauerstoff entzieht, um die Verbrennung zu unterstützen. Rauchfärbung und Musterung des Gefäßes entstehen nur da, wo es in Kontakt mit der Verbrennung ist. Es gibt natürlich zahlreiche Abweichungen in der Art und Weise und in welchem Ausmaß ein Gefäß geraucht ist, je nachdem, in welchem Winkel das Gefäß in die Sägespäne gesetzt wird. Wenn das Gefäß der Sägespäne entzogen wird, bevor der Brennvorgang beendet ist, wird der Rauchprozess unterbrochen. Solch ein Entzug muss mit großer Vorsicht unternommen werden, mit einer Rakuzange oder feuerfesten Handschuhen. Wenn irgendmöglich, vermeide ich die Rakuzange, weil sie das Gefäß beschädigen kann.

Eine zu schnelle Abkühlung ist nicht gut und ich lasse das Gefäß lieber noch 24 Stunden in der Öltrommel, nachdem der Brand beendet ist. Wenn das Gefäß wie beim Raku dem Brand entzogen wird, ist es ganz wichtig, den Abkühlungsvorgang zu steuern, indem man das Gefäß z.B. mit einer in Silberfolie eingeschlagenen keramischen Fasermatte abdeckt.

Erst wenn das Gefäß ganz abgekühlt ist, wasche ich es vorsichtig unter kaltem Wasser mit einem weichen Schwamm ab, um es zu säubern und die Färbung sichtbar zu machen. Das ist ein spannender Moment! Zum Schluss behandle ich die Oberfläche mit einer dünnen Schicht Wachspolitur, die den Glanz der polierten Oberfläche wie altes Leder herausbringt.

Meine Arbeitsweise ist sehr zeitraubend und intensiv und empfiehlt sich nicht für Leute, die mit Ungeduld ein schnelles Ergebnis erwarten. Aber meine Arbeit hat einen gleichmäßigen Rhythmus und kann hohe Anforderungen stellen, während sie gleichzeitig auch beruhigend wirkt.

Diam. 46 cm 1984

Height 25 cm
1986

Height 37 cm
1993

Height 28 cm
1993

Diam. 42 cm
1995

Height each 45 cm
1994

Diam. 15 cm
1992

Height 47 cm
1992

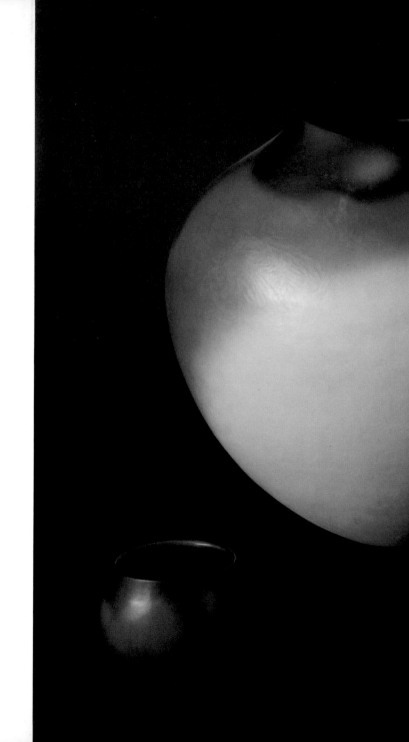

*Left to right* Diam. 12 cm, width 40 cm,
diam. 13 cm, diam. 40 cm, all 1994

*Left* Diam. 48 cm
1995

*Right* Height 52 cm
1995

Height 15 cm
1997

Height 41 cm
1997

*Left* Height 36 cm
1997

*Right* Height 39 cm
1996

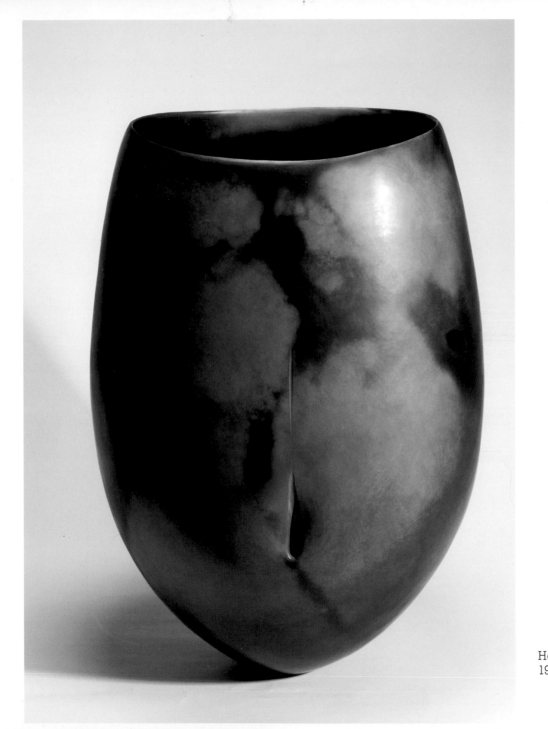

Height 35 cm     Height 41 cm
1998                  1999

Height 38 cm
1999

both sides
shown

Diam. 51 cm
1997

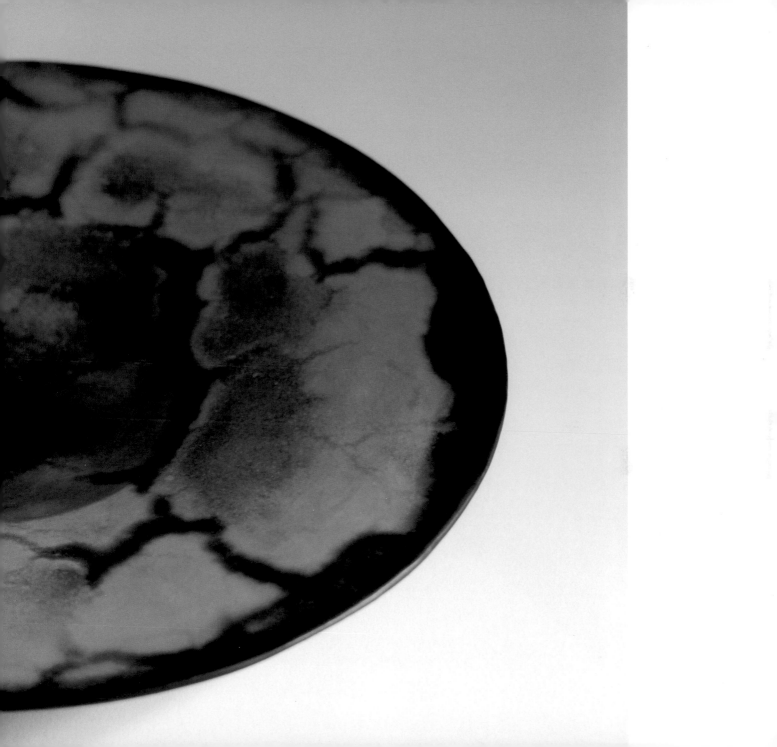

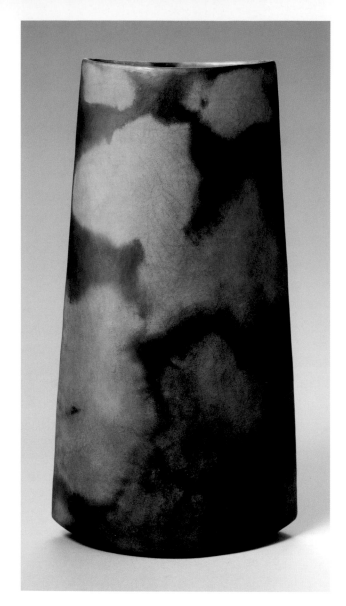

Height 41 cm
1999

*Below and right*
Height 20 cm
1999

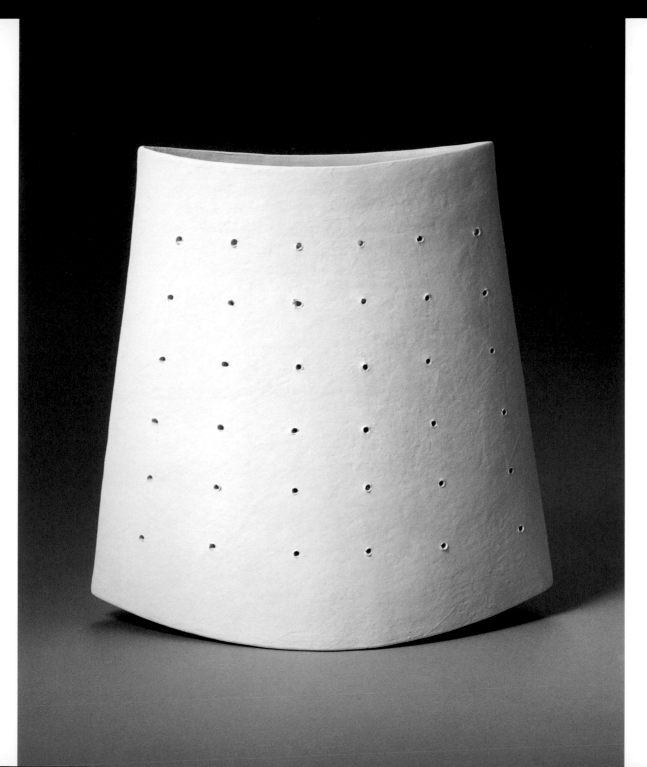

Height
42 cm
1999

Height
38 cm
1999

Width 35 cm
2000

Diam. 47 cm
2001

Height 36 cm
2001

Diam. 32 cm
2000

Height 41 cm
2001

Height 16 cm          Height 53 cm
2001                  2001

Height 35 cm
2001

Left
Diam. 42 cm
2001

Right
Height 25 cm
2001

Overleaf
Heights.
left to right:
33 cm,
37 cm,
42 cm,
42 cm,
45 cm,
all 2001

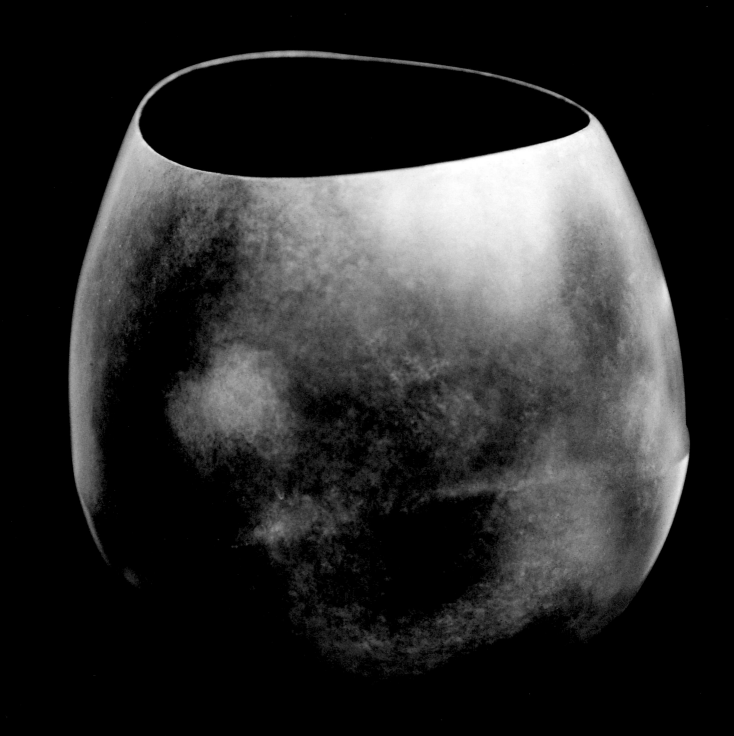

# Select Bibliography

*Zeitgenössisches Deutsches Kunsthandwerk,* Museum für Kunsthandwerk Frankfurt, Germany, 1984

*Aspekte 85 - Keramik aus England,* Keramion, Frechen, Germany, 1985

Peter Dormer, *The New Ceramics,* 1986

*Potters,* The Craftsmen Potters Association of Great Britain, 1989, 1992

Emmanuel Cooper/Cyril Frankel, *Gabriele Koch,* The Craft Centre and Design Gallery, Leeds, 1989

*Potters* 8th–12th Editions, Craft Potters Association, 1989–2000

Pat Carter, *A Dictionary of British Studio Potters,* 1990

*Keramik als Leidenschaft,* Museum Bellerive, Zurich, 1991

Frank Hamer, *The Potter's Dictionary of Materials and Techniques,* 1991, 1993

*Influential Europeans in Britsh Craft and Design,* Crafts Council, 1992

Martin Gayford, 'Feats of Clay', *Telegraph Magazine,* 26 June 1993

Tony Birks, *The Complete Potter's Companion,* 1993

Tony Birks, Low Tech: High Precision, *Ceramic Review,* No. 144, Nov/Dec. 1993

Karin Hessenberg, *Sawdust Firing,* 1994

Jane Perryman, *Smoke Fired Pottery,* 1995

Tony Birks, Sanfte Flamme, Langer Atem, *Keramik Magazin,* No. 4, 1995

Tony Birks, Gabriele Koch, *La Revue de la Céramique et du Verre,* No. 82, 1995

Edmund de Waal, Gabriele Koch, *Ceramic Series, Aberystwyth Arts Centre, No. 83* 1997

Betty Blandino, *Coiled Pottery,* 1997

Renée Fairchild, Gabriele Koch, *Ceramics Monthly,* Volume 48, 2000

Cyril Frankel, *Modern Pots, The Lisa Sainsbury Collection,* 2000

Tony Birks, Gabriele Koch, *La Revue de la Céramique et du Verre,* 120, 2001

Michael Hardy, *Handbuilding,* 2001

Height 35 cm
1998
bronze

# Gabriele Koch

1948     Born in Lörrach, South Germany
1967-73  University of Heidelberg, Degree in English, History, Political Science. Study and travels in Spain
1974-77  Camden Institute, London
1977-78  Postgraduate Certificate in Education, King's College, London
1979-81  Goldsmiths' College Diploma in Art & Design, Ceramics, London
1982     Crafts Council Setting-up Grant
1984     Crafts Council London Individual Grant
         Prize Biennale Internationale de Céramique d'Art, Vallauris

## Work in Public Collections

Museum für Kunsthandwerk, Frankfurt; Museum am Burghof, Lörrach; Badisches Landesmuseum, Karlsruhe; Shipley Art Gallery, Gateshead; Lotherton Hall, Leeds City Art Gallery; Towneley Hall Art Gallery & Museum, Burnley; Leeds Schools Art Loan Service; Sainsbury Collection, University of East Anglia; Contemporary Art Society, London; Wakefield Art Gallery; Bradford Art Gallery; Museum Bellerive, Zurich; European Investment Bank, Luxembourg; Aberdeen Art Gallery; Aberystwyth Arts Centre; City Museum & Art Gallery, Stoke-on-Trent; Victoria & Albert Museum, London; Liverpool Museum; Cleveland Studio Pottery Collection, Middlesbrough; Fitzwilliam Museum, Cambridge; Buckinghamshire County Museum, Aylesbury; The Eagle Collection, Gateshead; Lotte Reimers-Stiftung, Deidesheim.

## Solo Exhibitions

1984     Oliver & Pink, London
1986     The Crafts Centre and Design Gallery, Leeds
1987     Beaux Arts, Bath
1989     Sheila Harrison Fine Art, London
         The Craft Centre and Design Gallery, Leeds
1990     Beaux Arts, Bath
         Hannah Peschar Gallery, Ockley, Surrey
1991     The New Ashgate Galley, Farnham
         The Craft Centre and Design Gallery, Leeds
1992     Craft Showcase, Aberdeen Art Gallery
1993     Alpha House Gallery, Sherborne, Dorset
         Contemporary Ceramics, London
1994     Galerie L, Hamburg, Germany
1995     Alpha House Gallery, Sherborne, Dorset
         Hart Gallery, London
1996     Crafts Council Shop at V & A Museum, London
1997     Aberystwyth Arts Centre, Ceredigion
         Alpha House Gallery, Sherborne, Dorset
         Hart Gallery, London
1998     European Ceramics, Knaresborough
         Bluecoat Display Centre, Liverpool
         Studio 147, London
1999     Studio 147, London
2000     Gallery K, London
         Galerie am Brühl, Zell, Germany
         Studio 147, London
2001     Contemporary Applied Arts, London
         Galerie Pierre, Paris
         Studio 147, London
2002     Alpha House Gallery, Sherborne, Dorset
         Studio 147, London

## Mixed Exhibitions

1981     Ceramics 81, Seven Dials Gallery, London
1982     Goldsmiths' Gallery, London
1984     Biennale Internationale, Vallauris, France
         Black & White, British Crafts Centre, London
         Zeitgenössisches Deutsches Kunsthandwerk, Museum für Kunsthandwerk, Frankfurt/Kestner Museum Hanover

| 1985 | Aspekte 85, Keramion, Frechen, Germany |
| | Sculpture in a Wild Garden, Hannah Peschar Gallery, Surrey |
| | Art 16'85 Basle, Switzerland |
| | European Ceramics and Wall Textures, Fitzwilliam Museum, Cambridge Handbuilt Pots, Amalgam, London |
| | Galerie Gilbert, Remetschwiel, Germany |
| | Longstreet Gallery, Tetbury |
| 1986 | Christmas at CRE, CRE Ceramics, London |
| 1987 | Sculpture, Ceramics, Furniture, Hannah Peschar Gallery, Surrey |
| | Contemporary Ceramics, Sheila Harrison Fine Art, London |
| | Surface and Texture, Scottish Gallery, Edinburgh |
| 1988 | Sheila Harrison Fine Art, London |
| | A Celebration of Ceramics, Rufford Craft Centre, Newark |
| | Keramik aus England, Galerie für Englische Keramik Marianne Heller, Sandhausen |
| | Coiled Pots, Oxford Gallery, Oxford |
| | Ceramics by John Dunn, Gabriele Koch, David Roberts, Orleans House, Richmond |
| | Clayworks, Manchester City Art Gallery |
| 1989 | Keramik aus England, Galerie Handwerk, Munich, Germany |
| | Terrace Gallery, Worthing |
| | Potters 89, Craftsmen Potters Association, London |

| | |
|---|---|
| 1990 | British Ceramics Today, The New Ashgate Gallery, Farnham |
| | A Handful of Clay, Smith's Galleries, London |
| | New British Ceramics, Edinburgh College of Art |
| | Sheila Harrison Fine Art, London |
| | Lucie Rie, Hans Coper and their Pupils, University of East Anglia, Norwich |
| | Salt Glazed and Smoke Fired, Bluecoat Display Centre, Liverpool |
| | In the Eye of the Beholder, Prema Arts Centre, Dursley, Gloucestershire |
| 1990/91 | North of Watford Gap, Craftsmen Potters Association Touring Exhibition |
| 1991 | British Ceramics Today, New Ashgate Gallery, Farnham |
| | Keramik als Leidenschaft, Museum Bellerive, Zurich |
| | Ceramics, Peter Scott Gallery, Lancaster University, Lancaster |
| | Fire and Smoke, The South Bank Centre, London |
| | Hart Gallery, Nottingham |
| 1992 | A Collector's Choice, Terrace Gallery, Worthing |
| | Influential Europeans in British Craft and Design, Crafts Council Touring Exhibition |
| | Gifts to the Nation, Camden Arts Centre, London |
| | England to Barcelona, Catalan Craft Centre, Barcelona |
| | Poetics of Fire, Contemporary Ceramics, London |
| | Five Potters, The Craft Centre and Design Gallery, Leeds |
| 1993 | Handbuilt Ceramics, Rufford Craft Centre, Newark |
| | Burnished Pots, Oxford Gallery, Oxford |
| | European Ceramics, Maggie Barnes Ceramics, Knaresborough |
| | Handbuilt Ceramics, The Scottish Gallery, Edinburgh |
| 1994 | Studio Ceramics 94, Victoria & Albert Museum, London |
| | The Craft Centre and Design Gallery, Leeds |
| | International Fine Ceramics, Alpha House Gallery, Sherborne |
| 1995 | Out of this World, Crafts Council, London |
| | Primavera, Cambridge |
| | Winchester Gallery, Winchester |

| | |
|---|---|
| 1996 | 10 Years Crafts, The Scottish Gallery, Edinburgh |
| | New Ashgate Gallery, Farnham, Surrey |
| | 5th Anniversary Exhibition, On Line Gallery, Southampton |
| | A Summer Exhibition, Alpha House, Gallery, Sherborne |
| | Cups!, Garner Gallery, Glasgow |
| | Fired with Enthusiasm, Aberdeen Art Gallery, Aberdeen |
| 1997 | Ceramics 4 Collection, Woodbury Gallery, Woodbury |
| | The Royal Scottish Academy, Edinburgh |
| | Kaleidoscope, Contemporary Ceramics, London |
| | Summer Ceramics Selection, Hart Gallery, London |
| | Touching the Past, Contemporary Ceramics, London |
| 1998 | Cool Clay, Rufford Crafts Centre, Newark |
| | Mid-Cornwall Gallery, Par, St. Austell |
| | Rufford Crafts Centre, Newark |
| | Global Ceramics, Galerie Babel, Amsterdam, Holland |
| | International and Israeli Studio Ceramics, Tel Aviv |
| | Low fired Ceramics, Ruskin Gallery, Sheffield |
| | Special Focus Gabriele Koch, Contemporary Applied Arts, London |
| | The Discerning Eye, Mall Galleries, London |
| 1999 | 25 Years Already, Hugo Barclay Gallery, Brighton |
| | Burnt Earth, Contemporary Ceramics, London |
| | Come for a Potter, Artizana, Prestbury |
| | Objects of the Fire, Buckinghamshire Art Gallery, Aylesbury |
| | New Ashgate Gallery, Farnham, Surrey |
| 2000 | Burnished Pots, Oxford Gallery, Oxford |
| | Out of the Ashes, Craft in the Bay, Cardiff |
| 2001 | Loes and Reiner International Ceramics Gallery, Deventer, Holland |
| | International Fine Ceramics, Alpha House Gallery, Sherborne |
| | Rauchbrand, Kunstforum Kirchberg, Kirchberg, Switzerland |

Photography by Alphabet & Image, Stephen Brayne, Peter Kinnear and Heini Schneebeli.